Your Skin and Bones

Megan Duhamel

SCHOLASTIC INC.

NEW YORK • TORONTO • LONDON • AUCKLAND • SYDNEY
MEXICO CITY • NEW DELHI • HONG KONG • BUENOS AIRES

ISBN-13: 978-0-545-06097-4/ ISBN-10: 0-545-06097-4

Photos Credits:

Cover: © John-Francis Bourke/zefa/Corbis; title page: © Dan Dalton (RF)/Getty Images; contents page, from top: © Lisa Spindler Photography Inc./Getty Images, © Astrid & Hanns-Frieder Michler/Photo Researchers, Inc., © Tipp Howell/Getty Images; page 4: © Lisa Spindler Photography Inc./Getty Images; page 5: © Dorling Kindersley (RF)/Getty Images; page 6: © Frederic Lucano/Getty Images; page 7: © Ken Sherman/Jupiter Images; page 7, inset: © Ebby May/The Image Bank/Getty Images; page 8: © Astrid & Hanns-Frieder Michler/Photo Researchers, Inc.; page 9, left: © Thomas Northcut (RF)/Getty Images; page 9, right: © Purestock (RF)/Getty Images; page 10: © Edward Kinsman/Photo Researchers, Inc.; page 11: © 3D4Medical.com/Getty Images; page 12: © Stuart McClymont/Getty Images; page 13: © Tipp Howell/Getty Images; page 14, milk: © Davies and Starr/Getty Images; page 14, cheese: © Foodcollection (RF); page 14, yogurt: © Dorling Kindersley/Getty Images/Getty Images; page 14, broccoli: © Rosemary Calvert/Photographer's Choice/Getty Images; page 14, ice cream: © C Squared Studios (RF)/Getty Images; page 15: © Andersen Ross/Digital Vision/Getty Images; back cover: © John-Francis Bourke/zefa/Corbis.

Photo research by Dwayne Howard
Design by Holly Grundon

12 11 10 9 8 7 6 5 4 3 2   8 9 10 11 12 13/0

Printed in China
First printing, September 2008

Contents

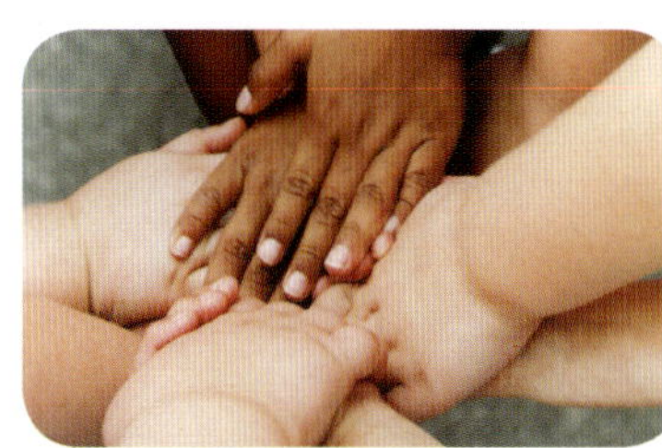

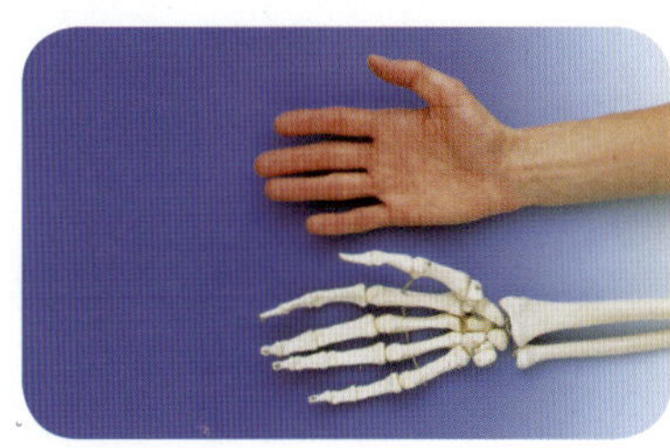

Chapter 1

Your Skin

Skin comes in many beautiful shades! Do you know what is beneath it? Bones! In this book, you will learn all about your skin and bones.

Layers of Skin

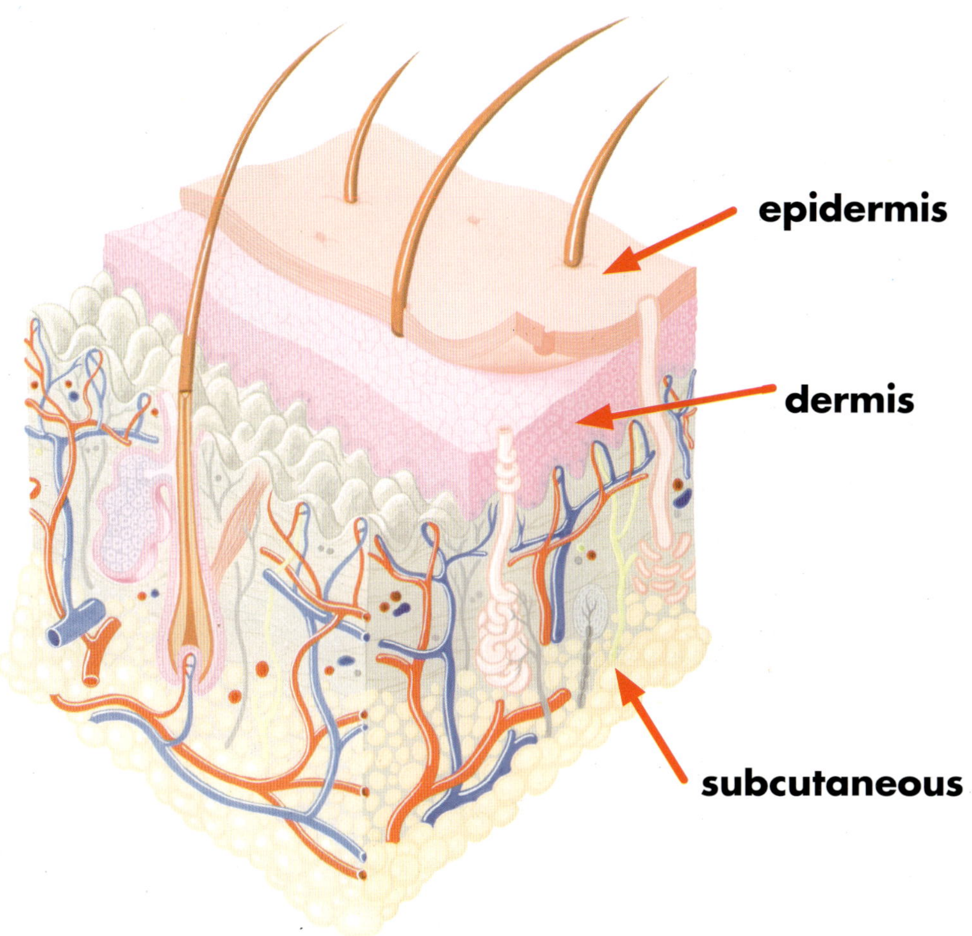

Let's start with your skin. It has three different **layers**. The layers help keep dirt and **germs** out of your body.

Fast Fact

Your skin is full of nerve endings that send messages to your brain like, "Brrrr! This icicle is cold!"

You use your skin to feel. Your skin lets you know if something is smooth or rough. Your skin warns you if something is cold or hot.

Your skin also helps you stay warm. Have you ever had goose bumps? That is your skin working to warm you up.

Chapter 2

Your Bones

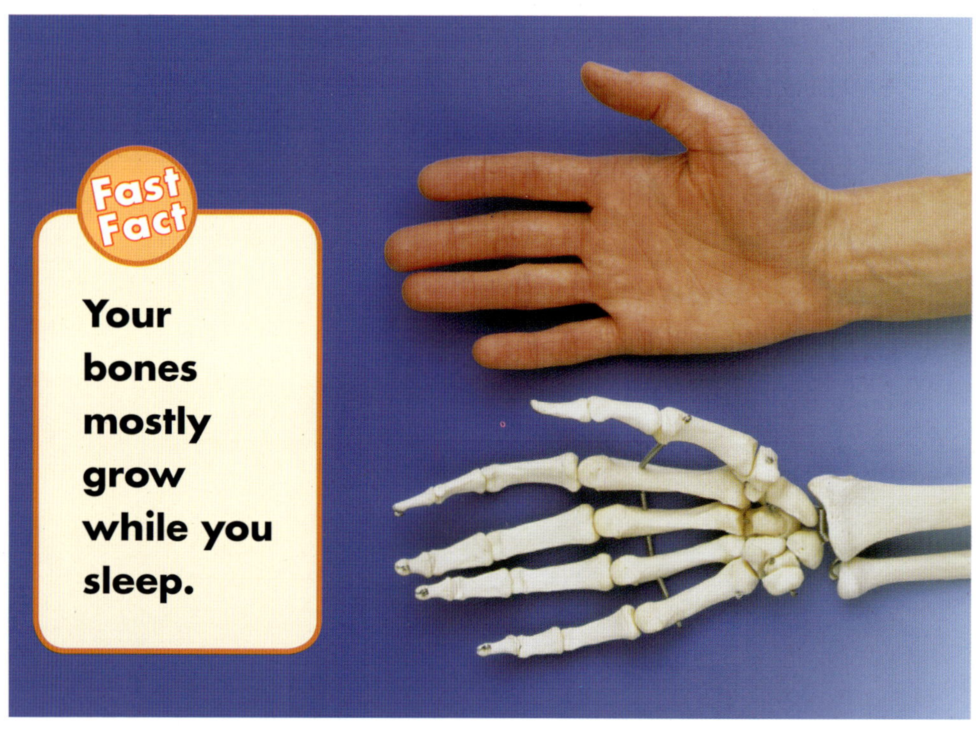

Squeeze your hand. Can you feel the bones beneath your skin? They are hard like rocks. But they are also alive. They grow as you grow.

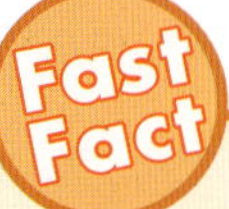

Your skull is made up of 28 different bones.

Outside

Inside

head

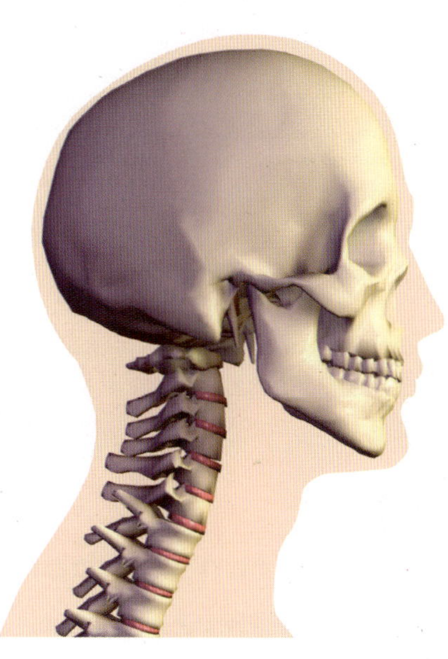

skull

Touch your head. Can you feel your **skull**? Your skull has an important job to do. It protects your brain.

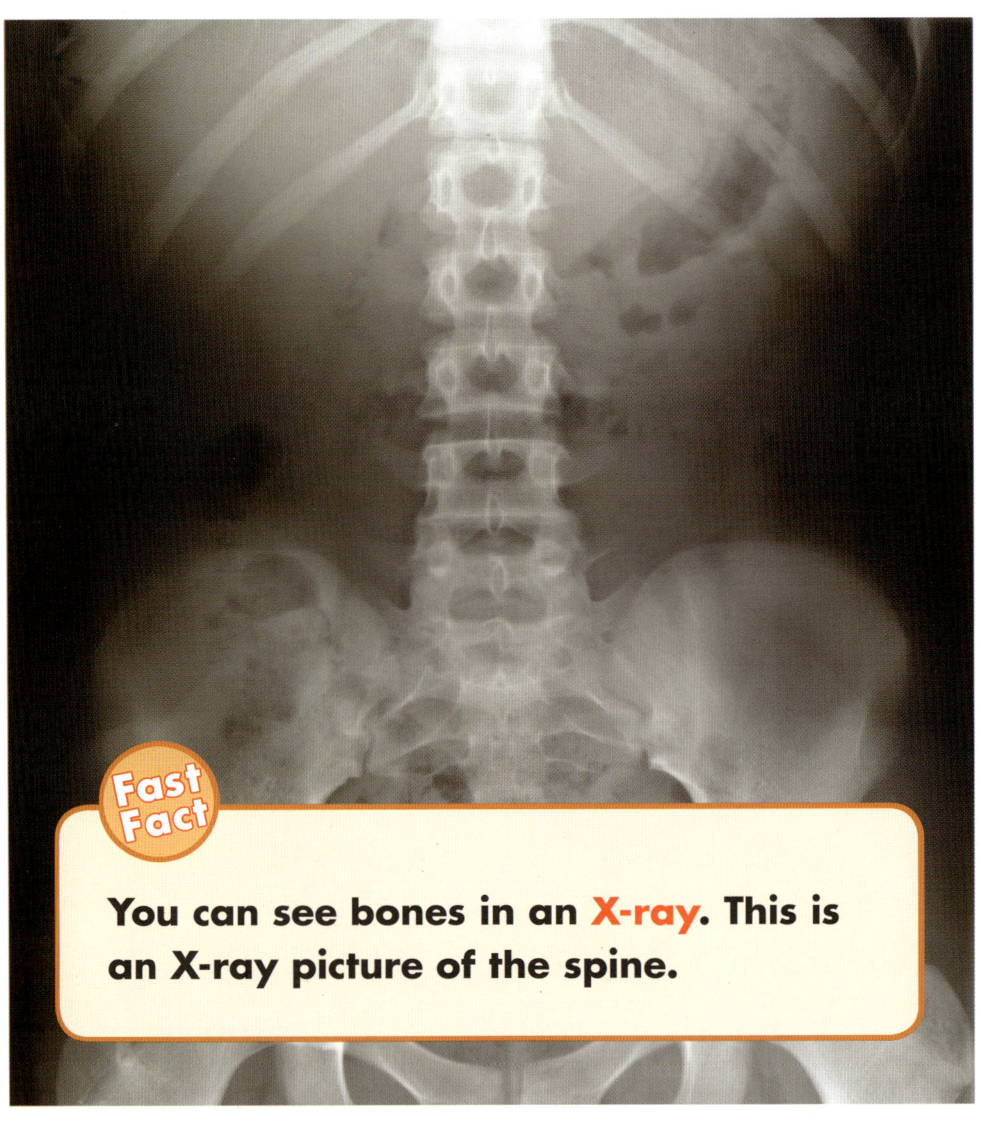

Fast Fact

You can see bones in an X-ray. This is an X-ray picture of the spine.

Run your finger along the middle of your back. Those little bumps are your **spine**. Your spine helps you bend over and stand up straight.

Skeleton

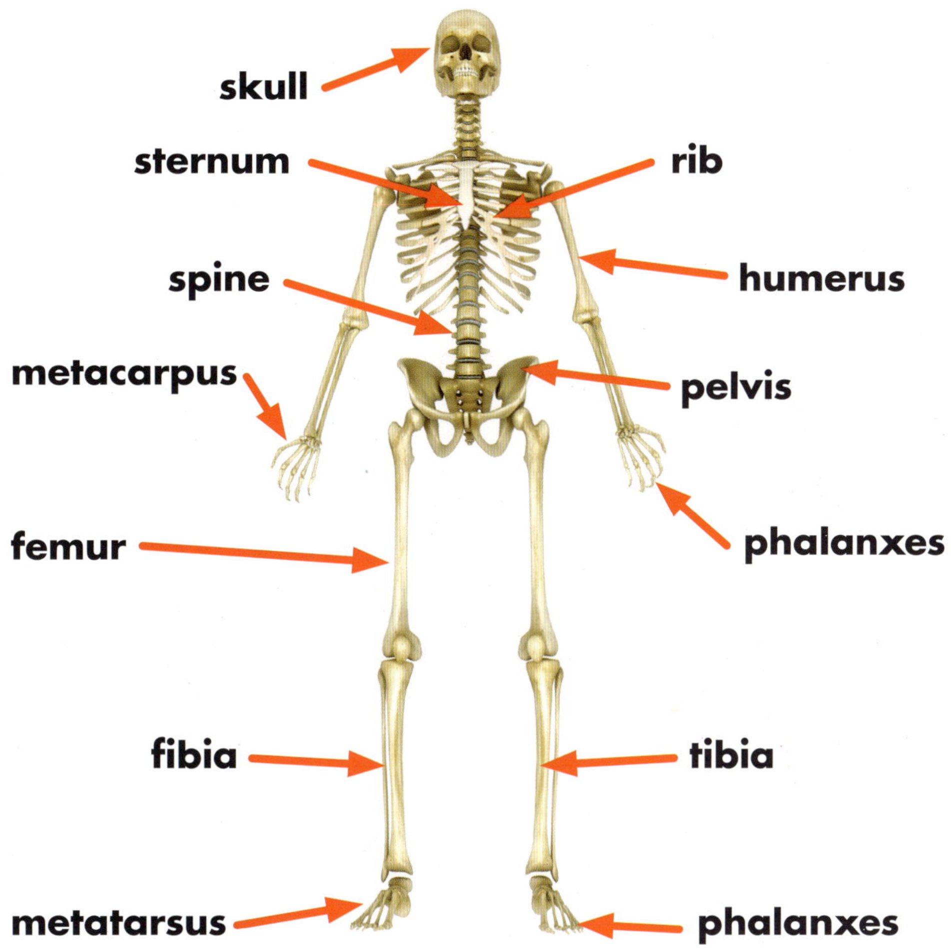

Your bones all fit together to make a **skeleton**. Each bone has a special name. Here are some of the names.

Chapter 3

Healthy Skin and Bones

Your skin keeps you covered and warm. So you need to take good care of it. How? Keep it clean!

Fast Fact

Band-Aids® were invented in the year 1920.

What should you do if you get a cut? First, clean it. Then, put on a bandage. This will help prevent it from getting **infected**.

Even though your bones are inside your body, you need to keep them healthy, too. What can you do? Eat and drink foods that have lots of **calcium**.

Fast Fact

Sports such as basketball, soccer, karate, jogging, jump-roping, and hiking help build strong bones, too.

Your skin and bones are important. Caring for them will help you grow strong!

Glossary

calcium (**kal**-see-uhm): a substance found in dairy products and some vegetables that builds strong bones

germs (**jurmz**): tiny organisms that cause disease

infected (in-**fekt**-id): made sick by germs or viruses

layer (**lay**-ur): a sheet or thickness of something, such as skin

nerve endings (**nurv end**ingz): bundles of fibers that send messages to the brain

skeleton (**skel**-e-ton): the framework of bones that supports and protects the body

skull (**skuhl**): the bony framework of the head

spine (**spine**): the backbone

X-ray (**eks** ray): special picture taken with a machine that can photograph the insides of things

Comprehension Questions

1. Can you share one fact about skin?
2. Can you share two facts about bones?
3. Can you name some ways to take care of your skin and bones?